# TAKING CARE OF YOUR

# FISH

Joyce Pope

Series consultant: Michael Findlay

Photographs by: Sally Anne Thompson
and R T Willbie/Animal Photography

Franklin Watts

New York   London   Toronto   Sydney

First Paperback Edition 1990
ISBN 0-531-15167-0

©1987 Franklin Watts
First published in Great
Britain in 1987 by
Franklin Watts
12a Golden Square
London W1

First published in the
United States of America
by
Franklin Watts Inc.
387 Park Avenue South
New York
N.Y. 10016

UK edition:
ISBN 0 86313 416 5
US edition:
ISBN 0–531–10192–4
Library of Congress
Catalog Card Number:
85–52088

**Designed by** Ben White
**Illustrated by** Hayward Art Group
**Additional photographs**
Heather Angel 16, 17, 28, 29
Jerzy Gawor 26, 27(L)

Acknowledgments
The photographers and publishers would like to thank
Mrs Anne Cosnette of Barrier Reef Aquatics,
Gloucester; The Widden Primary School, Gloucester,
and the families who took part in the photography for
this book.
    Special thanks are due to Brian Ward, author and
keen amateur aquarist, for his help in the preparation of
this book.

Printed in Belgium

# TAKING CARE OF YOUR

# FISH

## Contents

# Introducing pets

People like to keep pets. They can be an interesting part of our lives. It has been proved that caring for a pet can help anybody who is alone or unwell.

This is especially so for fish which can be looked after without much strength or agility.

▽ The fish that are kept in tanks come from many parts of the world, yet they can settle down well together. Their survival depends on you and you must try to give them the conditions that they need within the space of the tank.

# Fishkeepers' code

**1** Remember that a fish is not a toy, but a living creature.

**2** Although it lives in water, a fish has many needs and feelings, like hunger, contentment or fear, which are similar to yours.

**3** Remember that your fish depends on you for its survival. As it cannot tell you when something is wrong, you must watch it and care for it every day.

▽ Fish from the tropics need heated tanks, but a few kinds of fish can survive in cold water. Goldfish are the best known of these. They were first kept in China many years ago and there are now many different varieties for you to choose from.

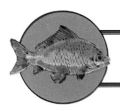 

Fish make ideal pets for anybody who lives in a town, where there is not much room to keep large, active pets that could bother other people.

Fish have the advantage that they are quiet and beautiful and they are not smelly. Many of the kinds that are kept as pets are not expensive.

◁ You can add interest to your tank by keeping several different kinds of fish together. You must get some that like to live near the bottom and others for the middle and upper level. The tank will not be overcrowded, though there may be quite a lot of fish in it.

Once the tank in which your fish live has been set up, they are quite easy to look after and cheap to feed. They move gracefully, and don't need to be exercised by you.

To some people, a disadvantage of a fish as a pet is that it cannot be handled and stroked. The fish itself cannot show you affection in the way that a dog or other mammal may do, although it may learn that certain sights or sounds mean that you are about to feed it. It may come to a particular corner of the tank and even poke its head out of the water.

△ Compared to human beings, or even to dogs or birds, fish are not very intelligent animals. But they can learn to know you and if they are rewarded with a tiny piece of food, they will get into the habit of coming toward you, when they see you. This may take some time, so do not be discouraged if they seem to learn very slowly – that is part of being a fish!

If we understand what a fish is, and how it lives, we then know how to give it the conditions it needs to survive well as a pet.

Like human beings, all fish are animals with backbones, though there are not many other obvious similarities, for fish are designed to spend all of their lives in water. Water is many times denser than the air in which we live, so in order to move easily fish have streamlined bodies.

△ Like all living animals fish feed, breathe, move and reproduce themselves. Like us, they can see, hear, smell, taste and feel. Their senses are often far more acute than ours.

Fish swim using side to side movements of the hind part of the body, which ends in a powerful tail fin. Other fins lie along the back or the underside of the fish and stabilize it in the water.

In addition, there are the pectoral (or shoulder) and pelvic (or hip) fins which are used for steering and braking as the fish swims. Fish breathe through their gills which take in oxygen which is dissolved in the water.

▽ When you watch your fish swim you will see that each has its own special way of doing so. Some dart about the tank; others swim lazily. They are able to hang in the water without falling through it because they have a sort of internal lifebuoy, called a swim bladder.

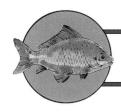

If you decide that you want to keep pet fish, the first thing to be sure of is that you have your parents' permission. The electricity bills will be slightly higher because of the cost of running a pump and possibly a heater in the fish tank. They may have to help you in other ways as well. You must find a suitable place in the house to put your fish tank.

It is difficult to keep a cold-water

▽ Setting up a fish tank can be costly, though if you do it properly your fish should cause you little further trouble or expense. A tank hood will stop things from falling in, or from jumping out.

Here are some pieces of equipment you will need: 1. Small plastic tank with hood. 2. Larger glass tank with hood. 3. Pump. 4. Water filter. 5. Lighting unit. 6. Thermometer and thermostat.

tank healthy in a warm house, although goldfish and paradise fish can live in indoors so long as the temperature does not change too fast. It is easier to keep warm water fish, as the water is heated to the right temperature all the time.

You should buy the biggest tank that you can afford. You can then keep more fish, and the larger size gives more stable conditions for the fish. A tank full of water weighs a great deal, so you may need a special stand for it. Put it in a place that is warm, but out of direct sunlight.

▽ You will need special equipment to clean your fish's home including 1. Scraper for removing algae from glass. 2. Siphon for picking up waste material from bottom of tank. 3. Glass cleaners. 4. Filtering system. 5. Net for removing fishes when you are doing a full spring-cleaning.

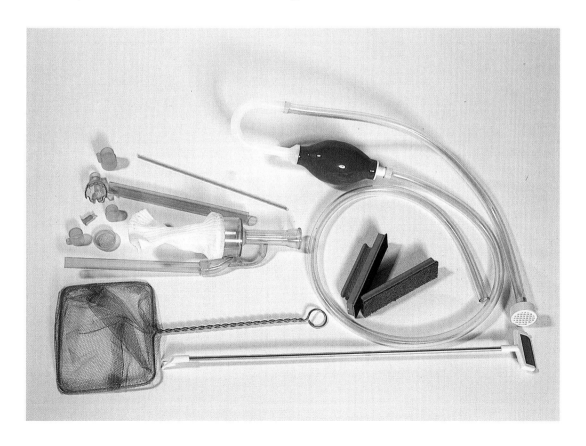

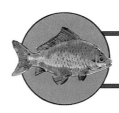

# Plants for your aquarium

The aquarium that you provide for your fish will form their whole world, so it is up to you to give them a pleasant living place. Besides making the tank more attractive to look at, plants give shelter, and sometimes food to the fish.

Plants are useful in other ways: as they grow, they use up some of the fishes' waste products and they

△ Plants for a cold water tank include;
1. Hornwort
2. Canadian pondweed
3. Vallisnaria
They should be held in position in the gravel with a weight, which will prevent your fish from moving them up.

release a little oxygen into the water.

There are many kinds of aquarium plants available in pet stores. Ask your pet dealer which ones are easily kept, and be sure that the fish you buy will not eat them. You should not collect plants from local streams or ponds, for you could bring in different disease organisms that would affect your pets.

For water plants free of disease you should go to a tropical fish store or a pet shop.

△ A warm water tank can be furnished with many sorts of plants.
Your aquarium store or pet shop will probably be able to advise you what to buy.

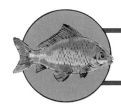

# Setting up your aquarium

▷ You should arrange the washed gravel in your tank so that it is thicker at the back than at the front. This way you will be able to see things better in the tank.

Your aquarium should be set up several days before you put any fish into it. This lets you be sure that the pump, lights, heater and filter are working properly. Don't forget to remove the chlorine, which is bad for fish, but present in tap water. Chlorine will disappear after water stands for several days, but your pet store can supply a chemical that removes it immediately.

You should get the gravel for the bottom of your tank from your

◁ When filling your tank put a dish on the gravel and pour the water into it. Otherwise the water will disturb the gravel.

aquarium dealer, who will advise you on how much you will need for the size of tank that you have bought. Before you put it into your tank, you should wash it. Put it in an old bowl and run water over it, then let it settle. Pour off the cloudy water containing silt and repeat the process until the water runs clear.

Do not use beach gravel, as the salt in it would be harmful to your freshwater pets.

When you finally put the gravel, plants and water into your tank, be sure that it is in its final position in the room – if you try to move it once it is full, it will almost certainly leak.

△ If need be, you can add extra plants at a later date. Bury the perforated pot in the gravel and weight it down with a stone. The roots will grow through and the plant will quickly establish itself.

# What sort of fish?

◁ A large aquarium can make a beautiful home for many kinds of fish. These have extra hiding places provided by a piece of log.

▽ Guppies, mollies and angel fish are among the fish living together in this tank.

Coldwater fish need cold, well aerated water, which is difficult to provide except in a large tank. So they are best kept in a pond out of doors. Goldfish or catfish can be kept without heat. So can the beautiful paradise fish, though they should never be mixed with other kinds of fish because they are aggressive.

There are far more kinds of tropical fish that can be kept. Many of these are beautiful, and have very

◁ There are many color varieties of high fin platies. They are easy to keep but need to eat a good deal of plant food.

▷ The tench is a European bottom-living cold water fish. It is very slimy and at one time was called the doctor fish, because people thought the slime could cure sick fish.

interesting life-histories. Some make nests for rearing their young, in others one or both of the parents act as nursemaids to the eggs and babies.

It is a good idea to visit a large aquarium or a big pet store to see as many kinds of fish as you can before you decide which ones you want.

Remember that when you buy young fish, they will grow larger. Some kinds of fish change color or shape as they get bigger and so may not be quite so attractive when they are full grown.

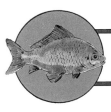

# Getting your fish

You should only get your fish after you have prepared a place for them to live.

Many kinds of fish normally live in groups or shoals, so it is better to buy several. The dealer will pick out the fish that you want and put them into a plastic bag with a little water.

They can live like this for a short time, but you should get them home

▽ At a big aquarium or pet shop you will be able to see lots of different kinds of fish and get advice as to which ones will do well together. You can choose the fish you want from a tank.

△ Your fish should be brought home well protected like this. If the weather is cold, the scarf should be tucked right over them.

as quickly as you can. They are best carried in a basket or box which has been lined with something warm, like a scarf. This will help to protect the fish from the cold and also from being bumped around. Most animals are more tranquil in the dark, so you should cover the bags well too, to make the journey less stressful for your pets.

Be sure to get the right number of fish for your aquarium. As a rule of thumb, stock the aquarium with no more than one inch of fish per gallon of water. Remember that fish will grow, so you may want to add fewer fish at first.

▷ You may choose to keep golden gouramis like these. They may take some time to settle in, and they can be aggressive toward other fish but eventually they may become very tame.

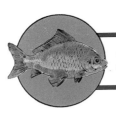
Even when you get your fish home, you should not rush to pour them into your aquarium. Just put the unopened bags containing the fish in the water. Because of the air that they contain, they will float. In half an hour or so the water in the bag will become as warm as the water in your tank. Then you can snip the bags open and let the fish swim out to begin to explore their new home.

◁ More fish are being added to an aquarium. The bag containing the new arrivals is floating on the surface of the water, and the fish in it will soon be liberated.

20

At first your fish will act as if they were frightened. They will dash for cover and may not come out, even to feed. They may even lose their color to some extent. But you must be patient. If you have bought healthy fish and they have the right conditions, they will soon settle in. Don't tap on the glass to try and make them swim into the open, this will frighten them more. Your patience will be rewarded, as your fish will be healthier with a quiet change of living conditions.

△ A well established aquarium. This one contains a variety of fish living peacefully together. The aquarium gives them a balanced environment with the right temperature, enough aeration, hiding and nesting places and food.

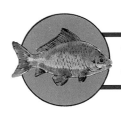

# Feeding your fish

In the wild, fish probably spend a good deal of their time looking for food, most of which consists of tiny creatures of various kinds. The food that you give to your pet fishes should be as near to their natural diet as possible.

They should be fed once or twice a day, but since the fish will not have to use up energy searching for their

△ There are many kinds of foods for fish available from your pet shop – most of these are in the form of flakes or pellets. Bottom-feeding fish, such as catfish, will eat pellets. Fish at all levels eat flake food.

food, the amount that you give them should be very small. Also, anything that is not eaten quickly is likely to foul the water and become a breeding ground for bacteria, which could cause illness to your fish.

The best food for your fish is dried food in the form of flakes or pellets. Always use flakes, for they will be eaten by all the fish that live at different levels in the water. (You can add some pellets for bottom feeders.) Many fish like live food, such as *daphnia* as a treat. Live food may be difficult to obtain, in which case freeze dried *daphnia* or brine shrimps may be used.

*Daphnia*

▷ Pet fish require very little food to remain healthy. An adult will probably help you to decide the right amount at first. A tiny pinch each day is enough for most fish, and if you give them more, it will not only be wasted, but may even cause disease.

23

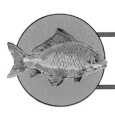

# Tank hygiene

Uneaten food, dead plants and other waste may build up in a tank, forming a brown sludge called mulm. This must be removed if your fish are to remain healthy.

Your filter should prevent too much mulm forming, but you must remove with a siphon any large

◁ You should hardly ever need to spring clean your aquarium. If you need to do so, you will find that it requires a lot of preparation. The fish must be moved using a small net, out into another tank while their usual home and its contents are cleaned, but they must be returned as soon as possible. Do not use bleach, or anything that might hurt the fish, when you clean the tank.

△ Normally all you need to do is to make sure that the filters are clean, and if any algae are growing on the glass you can scrape them off with a mounted blade like the one shown here.

fragments of waste, which are too big to be taken up by the filter.

If the tank gets too much direct light, you may find that tiny green plants called algae discolor the water and form a growth on the sides of the glass. You can buy scrapers to clean the glass, or use a nylon pot scourer. If the water is very green remove the fish and empty the tank. Refill the tank with water which has been standing for a few days.

To prevent the regrowth of the algae shade the side of the tank which is getting too much light. Use a piece of brown paper or cardboard. You could paint a water scene on it to add interest.

△ A siphon like this one is easy to use and very effective in picking up any uneaten pieces of food or other waste matter on the bottom of the tank. Make sure that the water siphoned out goes into the bucket! You will need to replace the water that you have removed.

25

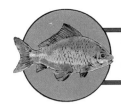

△ This goldfish is infested with the anchor worm parasite.

Because your aquarium is the home of far more animals than could live in such a space in the wild, you must watch your fish carefully for any signs of disease. An infection can spread very quickly in the small area of a tank, so any fish that seems to be unwell must be removed quickly and put into a "hospital tank" where it can be treated.

Some fish are bullies and may hurt some of the others. Usually the injuries are slight, but damage to a

◁ Fantails and orandas are prone to swim-bladder problems. They often swell up and lose their balance.

△ This fish is suffering from constipation. This can be cured by feeding it more greenstuff.

single scale can mean that a fungus infection may develop. This forms a fuzzy white growth over the fish's body. As soon as you see any sign of it, you should remove the fish to another tank, into which you have put a teaspoonful of sea salt per quart of water. This will kill the fungus quite quickly.

If a fish develops small white spots over its body, it may be suffering from a disease called white spot, or another called velvet. Your pet store will be able to provide you with the chemicals to put into the water of your tank to prevent the spread of these diseases.

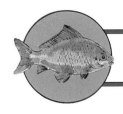

We are all used to the idea of bird or mammal watching, but many people do not realize that fish are just as interesting – and in many ways much easier – to watch. You will soon learn to recognize each of your fish, even those of the same kind.

If you watch your fish you can see their courtship. The males may become more brightly colored and dance in front of their mates.

Some, such as the paradise fish, do not need special conditions if they are to breed successfully. Many

▽ You can easily tell fancy goldfish apart, so you can learn to recognize their different behavior.

◁ Male sticklebacks in springtime have bright red undersides. Don't keep more than one male in a tank for they become very aggressive to other males.

kinds need a territory that they can keep for themselves and their families. They may have to be moved to another tank as they can become very aggressive toward other fish when they are setting up house.

You could keep a notebook to record what your fish do. This can make a good project into an exciting hobby.

△ Notice the way different kinds of fish act toward one another. The kinds of things that you can note in your fish project book are how they differ in their living places, their times of activity and the kinds of food that they like.

# Checklist

 **Before you buy:**

1 Make sure that your parents approve.
2 Decide what kinds of fish you want to keep.
3 Make sure that you have the right place to put the tank.
4 Get the tank, filter, gravel, plants, and if necessary, lights and heater.
5 Prepare the tank a few days before you get your fish.

 **Daily:**

1 Feed your fish.
2 Siphon up any large pieces of waste.
3 Check that none of your fish is showing any signs of illness. Remove it if it is.
4 Check that you have plenty of food for your fish and get more if need be.

 **Every three weeks or so:**

1 Clean your filter, if it is a box-type.
2 Remove some of the water from the tank, and replace it with new water that you have already dechlorinated.

 **Occasionally, or when needed:**

1 Spring-clean the tank, removing the fish to another tank while you do so. You will probably need an adult's help to do this.

# Questions and answers

**Q**  Can I keep coldwater fish and warmwater fish together?

**A**  No. Coldwater fish are really better in a pond out of doors and they should certainly not be put into a heated tank, nor can you put sea fish into freshwater, as this would kill them very quickly.

**Q**  How long can fish live?

**A**  Most small fish have short lives and cannot be expected to survive for more than 2 to 3 years.

**Q**  Can fish see colors?

**A**  Yes, most fish can see colors much as we do. They themselves may change color during the breeding season.

**Q**  Do all fish lay eggs?

**A**  No. A few fish lay live young and are called livebearers. Fish that lay eggs are called egglayers. In many cases the eggs are cared for by the parents and in some cases by the father.

**Q**  What should I do with my fish when I go away on holiday?

**A**  The best thing is to get your parents or neighbors to check each day that the pump and heater are working and to feed your fish. Make certain that they know not to overfeed the fish.

# Index